Table of Contents

Section No.	Section Title	Page No.
1.	"Beyond the Matrix" Introduction	3
2.	Author Introduction	5
3.	Learnings	7
4.	Part I: Unlearning the Matrix	9
	- Chapter 1: The Matrix Unveiled	10
	- Chapter 2: The Cost of Conformity	14
	- Chapter 3: Reclaiming Your Power	18
5.	Part II: Designing Your Escape	23
	- Chapter 4: Identifying Your Passions and Skills	24
	- Chapter 5: Validating Your Business Idea	29
	- Chapter 6: Building Your Business Foundation	33
6.	Part III: Navigating the Real World	38
	- Chapter 7: Overcoming Fear and Doubt	39
	- Chapter 8: Mastering the Art of Self-Discipline	44
	- Chapter 9: Building a Support Network	48
7.	Part IV: Thriving Beyond the Matrix	53
	- Chapter 10: Financial Freedom	54
	- Chapter 11: Living a Life of Purpose	59
	- Chapter 12: The Journey Continues	63
8.	Conclusion	67
9.	Resources	70

"Beyond the Matrix" Introduction

Core Message:

- "Beyond the Matrix" is a guide for those feeling trapped in the 9-to-5 grind. This book will guide you towards financial freedom, a life of purpose, and the ability to create your own reality.

- It challenges the conventional notion of job security and empowers readers to take control of their destiny by building their own businesses.

Key Points:

- The Illusion of Security: Exposes the limitations and risks of relying solely on a traditional job for financial stability.

- The Call to Awakening: Inspires readers to recognize their potential beyond the confines of the corporate world.

- Embracing the Red Pill: Encourages a conscious choice to step outside the comfort zone and pursue entrepreneurial freedom.

- Transformation: Guides readers through the process of unlearning limiting beliefs, identifying their passions and skills, validating business ideas, and building a sustainable enterprise.

- Empowerment: Provides practical advice, actionable steps, and motivational insights to overcome challenges and thrive as an entrepreneur.

Target Audience:

- Individuals feeling unfulfilled in their current jobs.

- Aspiring entrepreneurs seeking guidance and inspiration.

- Anyone who dreams of creating a life of greater freedom and purpose.

Whether you're a seasoned professional seeking a change or a budding entrepreneur eager to take the leap. It is time to break free from the illusion, embrace your entrepreneurial spirit, and embark on a journey of transformation.

"Open your eyes to a world of possibilities beyond the ordinary"

Author Introduction

Meet Your Guide: Logan

From Corporate Cubicle to Entrepreneurial Freedom:

Like many of you, I once found myself trapped in the matrix of the 9-to-5, feeling unfulfilled and dreaming of a life with more freedom and purpose. I traded my time and energy for a paycheck, but deep down, I knew there had to be a better way to live. I took the leap, faced my fears, and built a successful business doing what I love. It wasn't always easy, through years of trial and error, perseverance, self-discovery, and a willingness to learn, I successfully built a thriving business that allows me to live life on my own terms.

My Mission: Empowering Your Transformation:

Now, my passion lies in sharing the lessons I've learned and empowering others to break free from the matrix. I believe everyone has the potential to create a life of freedom and fulfillment, and I'm here to guide you every step of the way.

What I Bring to the Table:

- Real-world experience: I've walked the path from employee to entrepreneur, navigating the challenges and celebrating the victories.

- Actionable insights: I'll share practical strategies and proven tactics that you can implement immediately.

- Empathetic guidance: I understand the fears and doubts that come with stepping outside your comfort zone, and I'm here to offer support and encouragement.

"Unplug from the ordinary, plug into your potential"

Learnings

Unlock Your Entrepreneurial Potential

"Beyond the Matrix" is your roadmap to a life beyond the confines of the 9-to-5. Through its pages, you'll gain the knowledge, inspiration, and practical tools to:

- Unlearn the Matrix: Challenge societal norms and shed limiting beliefs that keep you trapped in the employee mindset.
- Discover Your True Self: Identify your passions, skills, and unique value proposition to build a business around what you love.
- Validate Your Ideas: Learn how to conduct market research and test your business concept to ensure its viability.
- Build a Solid Foundation: Master the essentials of business planning, goal setting, and branding to set yourself up for success.
- Navigate the Real World: Overcome fear and doubt, develop self-discipline, and build a supportive network to thrive as an entrepreneur.
- Achieve Financial Freedom: Implement strategies for managing your finances, investing wisely, and creating multiple income streams.
- Live a Life of Purpose: Align your business with your values, make a positive impact, and find true fulfillment.
- Embrace the Journey: Cultivate a mindset of lifelong learning, adaptability, and continuous growth as you evolve as an entrepreneur.

By the end of this book, you'll have the confidence and clarity to:

- Break free from the job illusion and create your own reality.
- Design a business that fuels your passions and provides financial security.
- Live a life of purpose, autonomy, and fulfillment.
- Leave a lasting legacy and inspire others to pursue their dreams.

"Knowledge is the spark, but action ignites the flame of transformation"

Part I: Unlearning the Matrix

- Chapter 1: The Matrix Unveiled

- Chapter 2: The Cost of Conformity

- Chapter 3: Reclaiming Your Power

CHAPTER ONE

The Matrix Unveiled - Challenge the norms, question the narratives. The path to truth begins with curiosity.

"The 9-to-5 is a cage, entrepreneurship is the key"

Unmasking the 9-to-5 Illusion: The Matrix of Modern Work

Imagine a world where most people spend the majority of their waking hours performing tasks they may not enjoy, for a company they may not fully believe in, all in exchange for a paycheck that barely covers their expenses. This is the reality for countless individuals trapped in the "9-to-5 matrix" – a system that often prioritizes conformity and compliance over individual passions and aspirations.

The Societal Conditioning: How We're Programmed for the Job Illusion

From a young age, we are subtly (and sometimes not-so-subtly) conditioned to believe that the path to success lies in securing a stable job, climbing the corporate ladder, and retiring with a pension. Our education system, media, and even our families often reinforce this narrative, instilling the belief that a traditional career is the only viable option for a secure and fulfilling life.

This societal conditioning can be so pervasive that we rarely question its underlying assumptions. We accept the 9-to-5 as the norm, even if it leaves us feeling unfulfilled, stressed, and financially constrained. But what if there's another way? What if there's a life beyond the matrix, where we can create our own rules and design a career that truly aligns with our passions and values?

The Myth of Job Security: The Fragile Foundation of the 9-to-5

One of the most powerful illusions perpetuated by the 9-to-5 matrix is the promise of job security. We're led to believe that a steady paycheck and benefits provide a safety net, protecting us from financial hardship and uncertainty. However, the reality is that job security is often an illusion.

In today's rapidly changing economy, companies are constantly restructuring, downsizing, and outsourcing jobs. Technological advancements are automating many tasks that were once performed by humans. Even the most loyal and dedicated employees can find themselves unexpectedly laid off, their sense of security shattered.

Moreover, relying solely on a single source of income can be incredibly risky. A sudden illness, injury, or economic downturn can quickly disrupt your financial stability. The 9-to-5 matrix can create a false sense of security, lulling us into complacency and preventing us from taking control of our financial future.

The Limitations of the 9-to-5: Trading Time for Money

Perhaps the most fundamental limitation of the 9-to-5 matrix is that it inherently restricts our freedom and potential. When we trade our time for money, we're essentially selling our most precious resource – our time on this planet. We're confined to a rigid schedule, often leaving little room for personal pursuits, family time, or creative endeavors.

Furthermore, the 9-to-5 often limits our earning potential. Our income is capped by our salary or hourly wage, regardless of how much value we create for our employer. We may have innovative ideas or untapped talents, but within the confines of the matrix, we may never have the opportunity to fully explore or monetize them.

The 9-to-5, can also stifle our creativity and passion. We may find ourselves performing repetitive tasks that don't challenge us or inspire us. Over time, this can lead to burnout, disillusionment, and a sense of being trapped in a meaningless cycle.

The Hidden Costs: The Price We Pay for Conformity

Beyond the financial and time constraints, the 9-to-5 matrix can take a toll on our physical and mental health. Long hours, stressful commutes, and demanding workloads can lead to chronic stress, anxiety, and even depression.

Moreover, the pressure to conform and fit in can suppress our individuality and authenticity. We may feel compelled to hide our true selves, fearing that our unique perspectives or ideas won't be accepted or valued. This can lead to a sense of disconnection and a lack of fulfillment in our work.

The Opportunity Cost: What We Sacrifice by Staying in the Matrix

Perhaps the most significant cost of staying within the 9-to-5 matrix is the opportunity cost – the potential experiences, achievements, and personal growth that we miss out on by not pursuing our own path.

Imagine the possibilities if you could dedicate your time and energy to building something of your own, something that truly excites and inspires you. Imagine the freedom to set your own schedule, work from wherever you want, and create a life that aligns with your values and aspirations.

By remaining in the matrix, we sacrifice the chance to discover our true potential, to make a meaningful impact on the world, and to live a life of purpose and fulfillment.

Breaking Free: The Path to Truth and Self-Discovery

The first step to breaking free from the 9-to-5 matrix is to challenge the norms and question the narratives that have been ingrained in us since childhood. It's about cultivating curiosity, seeking alternative perspectives, and daring to imagine a different reality.

This journey of self-discovery may not be easy. It will require courage, resilience, and a willingness to step outside your comfort zone. But the rewards are immeasurable.

By breaking free from the matrix, you can:

- **Achieve financial independence:** Build a business that generates income on your terms, freeing you from the reliance on a single paycheck.

- **Design your dream lifestyle:** Create a schedule that allows you to prioritize your health, relationships, and personal passions.
- **Pursue your passions:** Build a career around your unique talents and interests, doing work that truly excites and fulfills you.
- **Make a meaningful impact:** Use your skills and resources to contribute to the world in a way that aligns with your values.
- **Live a life of purpose:** Discover your true calling and create a life that is rich in meaning and satisfaction.

Remember:

- **The 9-to-5 is not the only path:** There are countless ways to create a fulfilling and successful life. Don't be afraid to explore alternative options.
- **Question everything:** Don't blindly accept the status quo. Challenge assumptions, seek out diverse perspectives, and form your own opinions.
- **Embrace curiosity:** Cultivate a thirst for knowledge and a willingness to learn. The more you explore, the more you'll discover about yourself and the world around you.
- **Your potential is limitless:** Don't let societal expectations or limiting beliefs hold you back. You have the power to create your own reality.
- **The journey begins with a single step:** Take that first step towards breaking free from the matrix. It may be scary, but it's also incredibly empowering.

The journey begins with a single question: Are you ready to break free from the matrix and create your own reality?

In the following chapters, we will explore the steps you can take to escape the 9-to-5 illusion, design your own path, and build a life of freedom, purpose, and abundance. The path to truth begins with curiosity, and the journey to a fulfilling life starts with a single step.

CHAPTER TWO

The Cost of Conformity - Awaken from the slumber of complacency. Discover the vibrant life that awaits beyond the illusion.

"Don't just dream your reality, create it"

High Price of Playing it Safe: Unveiling the Hidden Costs of the 9-to-5

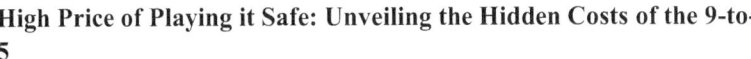

In the previous chapter, we peeled back the layers of the 9-to-5 matrix, revealing the societal conditioning and illusory promises that keep so many trapped in unfulfilling careers. Now, it's time to delve deeper and examine the true cost of conformity—the sacrifices we make, both tangible and intangible, by remaining within this system.

Financial Sacrifice: The Illusion of Stability

At first glance, the 9-to-5 seems to offer a sense of financial security. A regular paycheck, health insurance, and a retirement plan can create the illusion of stability. However, this stability often comes at a high price.

- **Limited Earning Potential:** Your income is capped by your salary or hourly wage, regardless of your skills, talents, or the value you create for your employer. You may be capable of achieving much more, but within the confines of the matrix, your earning potential is restricted.

- **The Rat Race:** The constant pressure to keep up with rising living costs, pay off debts, and save for the future can lead to a perpetual feeling of being on a treadmill, always striving for more but never quite reaching a point of true financial freedom.

- **Lifestyle Inflation:** As your income increases, so do your expenses. You may find yourself upgrading your lifestyle, buying a bigger house, a newer car, and indulging in more luxuries. This can create a cycle of dependency on your job, making it even harder to break free from the matrix.

- **The Golden Handcuffs:** The benefits and perks associated with your job can become "golden handcuffs," tying you to a career that may no longer fulfill you. The fear of losing these benefits can prevent you from taking risks and pursuing opportunities that could lead to greater financial rewards and personal satisfaction.

Personal Sacrifice: Time, Health, and Fulfillment

The 9-to-5 matrix demands a significant portion of your time and energy. Long hours, stressful commutes, and demanding workloads can leave you with little time for personal pursuits, hobbies, or spending quality time with loved ones.

- **Time Poverty:** The average full-time employee spends approximately 40 hours per week at work, not including commute time or additional hours spent on work-related tasks outside of the office. This leaves precious little time for personal growth, relaxation, or pursuing your passions.

- **Health Concerns:** Chronic stress, lack of sleep, and sedentary lifestyles associated with many 9-to-5 jobs can contribute to a host of health problems, including heart disease, obesity, and mental health issues.
- **Emotional Toll:** Feeling unfulfilled in your work can lead to a sense of apathy, frustration, and even depression. The constant pressure to perform and meet deadlines can take an emotional toll, leaving you feeling drained and unmotivated.
- **Strained Relationships:** The demands of your job can strain your relationships with family and friends. You may miss important events, struggle to maintain healthy communication, or feel guilty for not being more present.

The Opportunity Cost: Dreams Deferred

Perhaps the most profound cost of conformity is the opportunity cost—the dreams and aspirations you put on hold while you remain within the matrix.

- **Unexplored Passions:** You may have hidden talents, creative ideas, or entrepreneurial ambitions that you never get the chance to explore. The 9-to-5 can become a comfortable cage, preventing you from taking risks and pursuing your true passions.
- **Personal Growth Stagnation:** When your focus is solely on your job, you may neglect your personal development and growth. You may miss out on opportunities to learn new skills, expand your knowledge, or challenge yourself in ways that could lead to greater fulfillment.
- **Missed Adventures:** The 9-to-5 can limit your ability to travel, explore new cultures, or embark on life-changing experiences. The fear of taking time off or disrupting your career trajectory can keep you tethered to a routine that may not align with your true desires.
- **Regret and Resentment:** As time passes, you may start to feel a sense of regret for the opportunities you missed and the dreams you deferred. This can lead to resentment towards your job, your employer, and even yourself for not having the courage to break free sooner.

The Wake-Up Call: Recognizing the Need for Change

The first step towards breaking free from the matrix is recognizing the true cost of conformity. It's about acknowledging the sacrifices you're making, both financially and personally, and realizing that there is a vibrant life waiting for you beyond the illusion of the 9-to-5.

Once you awaken from the slumber of complacency, you can start to question the status quo and explore alternative paths. You can begin to envision a life where you're in control of your time, your finances, and your destiny.

Breaking the Chains: Embracing Your Entrepreneurial Spirit

Breaking free from the matrix requires courage, resilience, and a willingness to embrace your entrepreneurial spirit. It's about taking ownership of your life, your career, and your future.

The journey may not be easy, but the rewards are immeasurable. By stepping outside your comfort zone and pursuing your passions, you can create a life of freedom, purpose, and abundance.

Remember:

- **You are not alone:** Many others have successfully escaped the 9-to-5 and built thriving businesses. You have the potential to do the same.
- **The time is now:** Don't wait for the "perfect" moment to make a change. The sooner you start, the sooner you can begin creating the life you truly desire.
- **Embrace the journey:** The path to entrepreneurship is filled with challenges and learning opportunities. Embrace the journey, stay curious, and never stop growing.

In the next chapter, we'll explore how to reclaim your power and shift your mindset from employee to entrepreneur. It's time to awaken from the slumber of complacency and discover the vibrant life that awaits beyond the illusion.

CHAPTER THREE

Reclaiming Your Power - Believe in your boundless potential. The power to create your own reality lies within you.

" Embrace the unknown, for that's where growth lies"

Employee to Entrepreneur: Shifting Your Mindset

 In the previous chapters, we exposed the illusions and limitations of the 9-to-5 matrix, revealing the high cost of conformity and the sacrifices we make by remaining within this system. Now, it's time to embark on a journey of transformation—a journey from employee to entrepreneur, from complacency to empowerment.

This chapter is about reclaiming your power, shifting your mindset, and cultivating the entrepreneurial spirit that lies dormant within you. It's about recognizing your boundless potential and embracing the belief that you have the power to create your own reality.

Unlearning the Old Paradigm: Challenging Limiting Beliefs

The first step in reclaiming your power is to unlearn the old paradigm—the deeply ingrained beliefs and assumptions that have shaped your perception of work and success. These beliefs, often instilled in us from a young age, can act as mental barriers, preventing us from seeing the possibilities that exist beyond the 9-to-5 matrix.

Some common limiting beliefs include:

- **"I'm not smart enough/talented enough/experienced enough to start my own business."**
- **"I need a stable job to be financially secure."**
- **"Entrepreneurship is too risky."**
- **"I don't have the resources or connections to succeed."**
- **"I'm not cut out to be a leader."**

These beliefs, while seemingly harmless, can be incredibly powerful in shaping our actions and decisions. They can hold us back from taking risks, pursuing our passions, and ultimately creating the life we truly desire.

To break free from these limiting beliefs, it's essential to challenge them with evidence and logic. Ask yourself:

- **"Is this belief based on facts or fear?"**
- **"Are there examples of people who have overcome similar challenges and achieved success?"**
- **"What are the potential rewards of stepping outside my comfort zone and pursuing my dreams?"**

By actively challenging and reframing these limiting beliefs, you can create space for new possibilities and empower yourself to take action.

Cultivating an Entrepreneurial Mindset: Embracing Growth and Resilience

The entrepreneurial journey is not for the faint of heart. It requires a unique mindset—one that embraces challenges, welcomes uncertainty, and thrives on continuous learning and growth.

Here are some key characteristics of an entrepreneurial mindset:

- **Vision:** The ability to see beyond the present and envision a future where your dreams become reality.
- **Passion:** An unwavering enthusiasm for your business idea and a deep desire to make a positive impact.
- **Resilience:** The capacity to bounce back from setbacks, learn from failures, and keep moving forward.
- **Adaptability:** The willingness to embrace change, pivot when necessary, and constantly evolve your strategies.
- **Resourcefulness:** The ability to find creative solutions to problems, even with limited resources.
- **Self-belief:** A deep-seated confidence in your abilities and a unwavering commitment to your vision.

Cultivating an entrepreneurial mindset is an ongoing process. It requires self-awareness, reflection, and a willingness to step outside your comfort zone. Here are some strategies to help you develop this mindset:

- **Surround yourself with positive influences:** Seek out mentors, role models, and communities of like-minded entrepreneurs who can inspire and support you on your journey.
- **Embrace continuous learning:** Read books, listen to podcasts, attend workshops, and invest in your personal and professional development.
- **Practice self-care:** Prioritize your physical and mental health, ensuring you have the energy and resilience to navigate the ups and downs of entrepreneurship.
- **Celebrate small wins:** Acknowledge your progress and celebrate your achievements, no matter how small they may seem.

- **Cultivate a growth mindset:** Embrace challenges as opportunities for learning and view failures as stepping stones to success.

Embracing Self-Belief: Unleashing Your Inner Power

At the core of reclaiming your power is embracing self-belief—the unwavering confidence in your abilities and your potential to achieve your goals.

Self-belief is not about arrogance or ego; it's about recognizing your inherent worth and trusting your intuition. It's about silencing the inner critic and embracing the voice that tells you, "You can do this."

Here are some ways to cultivate self-belief:

- **Practice positive self-talk:** Replace negative thoughts with affirmations and empowering statements.
- **Visualize your success:** Imagine yourself achieving your goals and living the life you desire.
- **Focus on your strengths:** Identify your unique talents and skills and leverage them to your advantage.
- **Take action:** Don't wait for the perfect moment or for all the answers to fall into place. Start taking small steps towards your goals today.
- **Surround yourself with supportive people:** Connect with individuals who believe in you and encourage your dreams.

From Vision to Reality: Taking Action

Reclaiming your power is not just about changing your mindset; it's about taking action. It's about translating your dreams and aspirations into tangible steps that move you closer to your goals.

Here are some key actions you can take to start creating your own reality:

- **Define your vision:** What kind of life do you want to create? What are your passions and values? What impact do you want to make on the world?
- **Set clear goals:** Break down your vision into smaller, achievable goals that you can track and measure.
- **Develop a plan:** Create a roadmap for achieving your goals, outlining the steps you need to take and the resources you'll need to acquire.
- **Take action:** Start implementing your plan, even if it's just one small step at a time.

- **Stay persistent:** Don't give up on your dreams, even when faced with challenges or setbacks. Remember, the path to success is rarely a straight line.

Embrace the Journey: The Power of Transformation

Reclaiming your power and breaking free from the matrix is a journey of transformation—a journey of self-discovery, growth, and empowerment. It's about shedding old beliefs, embracing new possibilities, and creating a life that is authentically yours.

As you embark on this journey, remember:

- **You are capable of amazing things.** You have the power to create your own reality and achieve your wildest dreams.

- **The journey is just as important as the destination.** Embrace the challenges, celebrate the victories, and learn from every experience.

- **You are not alone.** There are countless others who have walked this path before you. Seek out mentors, connect with like-minded individuals, and build a support network to help you along the way.

In the following chapters, we will delve deeper into the practical steps you can take to design your escape from the 9-to-5 matrix and build a thriving business that aligns with your passions and values. But for now, take a moment to reflect on the power that lies within you. Believe in your boundless potential and embrace the journey of transformation that awaits.

Part II: Designing Your Escape

- **Chapter 4: Identifying Your Passions and Skills**

- **Chapter 5: Validating Your Business Idea**

- **Chapter 6: Building Your Business Foundation**

CHAPTER FOUR

Identifying Your Passions and Skills - Unleash your inner fire. Embrace your passions and skills to forge a path that is uniquely yours.

"Your passions are your compass, follow them fearlessly"

Embarking on the Journey of Self-Discovery: Finding Your North Star

In the previous chapters, we've explored the limitations of the 9-to-5 matrix and the importance of cultivating an entrepreneurial mindset. Now, it's time to embark on a journey of self-discovery, to uncover your passions and skills and align them with a business that sets your soul on fire.

The Power of Passion: Fueling Your Entrepreneurial Drive

Passion is the driving force behind any successful endeavor. It's the spark that ignites your motivation, the fuel that keeps you going when faced with challenges, and the compass that guides you towards your true purpose.

When you're passionate about what you do, work doesn't feel like work. It becomes a source of joy, fulfillment, and creative expression. Your enthusiasm is contagious, inspiring others and attracting opportunities.

But how do you identify your passions? Here are some key questions to ask yourself:

- **What activities make time fly by?** What are you doing when you're so engrossed that you lose track of time?
- **What topics do you love learning about?** What subjects or areas of interest pique your curiosity and keep you engaged?
- **What problems do you want to solve?** What challenges in the world ignite your desire to make a difference?
- **What brings you a sense of joy and fulfillment?** What activities or experiences leave you feeling energized and satisfied?
- **What are your natural talents and strengths?** What comes easily to you, or what do others compliment you on?

Reflecting on these questions can help you uncover the activities, interests, and causes that truly ignite your passion. Once you've identified your passions, you can begin to explore how they might translate into a fulfilling and profitable business.

Unveiling Your Skills: Recognizing Your Unique Talents

Skills are the tools you use to navigate the world and achieve your goals. They can be learned, developed, and honed over time through practice, experience, and education.

Identifying your skills is essential for building a successful business. It allows you to leverage your strengths, offer valuable services or products, and stand out in the marketplace.

Here are some strategies for uncovering your skills:

- **Reflect on past experiences:** Consider your previous jobs, volunteer work, hobbies, and personal projects. What tasks did you enjoy? What challenges did you overcome? What accomplishments are you most proud of?
- **Seek feedback from others:** Ask friends, family, colleagues, and mentors for their honest assessment of your strengths and talents.
- **Take online assessments:** Several online tools and assessments can help you identify your skills and personality traits.
- **Experiment and explore:** Try new activities, take courses, and volunteer your time to discover hidden talents and interests.

Remember, skills can be both hard and soft.

- **Hard skills** are specific, teachable abilities, such as coding, writing, graphic design, or accounting.
- **Soft skills** are more general and transferable, such as communication, leadership, problem-solving, and adaptability.

Both hard and soft skills are valuable in the entrepreneurial world. By recognizing and leveraging your unique combination of skills, you can create a business that capitalizes on your strengths and sets you apart from the competition.

Finding Your "Ikigai": The Intersection of Passion, Skills, Mission, and Vocation

The Japanese concept of "Ikigai" refers to the intersection of four key elements:

1. **What you love (your passion)**
2. **What you're good at (your skills)**
3. **What the world needs (your mission)**
4. **What you can be paid for (your vocation)**

Finding your Ikigai is about discovering the sweet spot where your passions, skills, mission, and vocation align. When you're operating within your Ikigai, you're not just building a business; you're living a life of purpose, fulfillment, and contribution.

Tips for Finding Your Ikigai:

- **Reflect on your values and priorities:** What matters most to you in life? What kind of impact do you want to make on the world?

- **Explore different possibilities:** Don't be afraid to experiment and try new things. The more you explore, the closer you'll get to discovering your Ikigai.
- **Seek feedback and guidance:** Talk to mentors, coaches, or trusted friends who can offer insights and support.
- **Be patient and persistent:** Finding your Ikigai is a journey, not a destination. It takes time, self-reflection, and a willingness to explore different paths.

Aligning Passions with Profitable Ventures: Turning Your Dreams into Reality

Once you've identified your passions and skills, it's time to explore how you can leverage them to create a profitable business. This involves:

- **Brainstorming business ideas:** Generate a list of potential business ideas that align with your passions and skills. Don't censor yourself at this stage; let your creativity flow.
- **Conducting market research:** Evaluate the demand for your potential business ideas. Is there a market for your products or services? Who are your target customers? What are their needs and pain points?
- **Identifying your unique value proposition:** What sets you apart from the competition? What unique skills or perspectives can you offer?
- **Creating a business plan:** Outline your business goals, target market, marketing strategy, financial projections, and operational plan.

Remember, not every passion or skill will translate directly into a profitable business. However, by being creative, resourceful, and persistent, you can find ways to monetize your talents and create a business that allows you to do what you love while making a living.

Embracing the Journey: Forging Your Unique Path

The process of identifying your passions and skills is a journey of self-discovery. It's about uncovering your true potential, embracing your unique talents, and creating a life that is authentically yours.

As you embark on this journey, remember:

- **Be patient with yourself:** Self-discovery takes time. Don't expect to have all the answers overnight.
- **Embrace the unknown:** Be open to new experiences, challenges, and opportunities.
- **Trust your intuition:** Listen to your gut feeling and follow your heart.

- **Celebrate your progress:** Acknowledge your achievements, no matter how small, and use them as motivation to keep moving forward.

- **Never give up on your dreams:** The path to success may not always be easy, but with passion, perseverance, and a clear vision, you can achieve anything you set your mind to.

By unleashing your inner fire and embracing your passions and skills, you can forge a path that is uniquely yours, a path that leads to a life of freedom, fulfillment, and entrepreneurial success.

CHAPTER FIVE

Validating Your Business Idea -Dare to be different. Challenge the status quo and let your innovative spirit shine.

"Validate your vision, then build your empire"

Passion to Profit: Turning Your Dream into a Sustainable Reality

From You've unearthed your passions, honed your skills, and perhaps even discovered your Ikigai. Now, armed with a treasure trove of business ideas, it's time to take the crucial step of validating those ideas. This chapter is your guide to navigating the exciting yet often daunting process of transforming your entrepreneurial vision into a viable and thriving business.

The Importance of Validation: Avoiding the Pitfalls of Assumption

It's easy to fall in love with an idea, especially when it aligns with your passions. However, passion alone doesn't guarantee success. Countless businesses fail each year because they were built on assumptions rather than solid evidence.

Validating your business idea involves gathering data and feedback to ensure there's a genuine need for your product or service in the marketplace. It's about minimizing risks, maximizing opportunities, and setting yourself up for long-term success.

Conducting Market Research: Unveiling the Needs and Desires of Your Target Audience

Market research is the cornerstone of idea validation. It involves gathering information about your target market, their needs, preferences, and behaviors. By understanding your potential customers, you can tailor your offering to meet their specific demands and create a compelling value proposition.

Here are some key market research methods:

- **Surveys and Questionnaires:** Create online or offline surveys to gather quantitative and qualitative data about your target market. Ask questions about their pain points, preferences, and willingness to pay for your product or service.

- **Interviews and Focus Groups:** Conduct in-depth interviews or focus groups with potential customers to gain deeper insights into their needs, motivations, and decision-making processes.

- **Observational Research:** Observe your target market in their natural environment to understand their behaviors and interactions with similar products or services.

- **Competitive Analysis:** Analyze your competitors' strengths, weaknesses, pricing strategies, and marketing tactics to identify opportunities for differentiation.

- **Secondary Research:** Utilize existing data and reports from industry publications, government agencies, and market research firms to gain a broader understanding of the market landscape.

Identifying Your Target Audience: Who Are You Serving?

Understanding your target audience is essential for creating a product or service that resonates with them. It's about identifying the specific group of people who are most likely to benefit from your offering and tailoring your marketing and communication efforts accordingly.

Here are some factors to consider when defining your target audience:

- **Demographics:** Age, gender, location, income level, education, occupation, etc.
- **Psychographics:** Lifestyle, interests, values, personality traits, etc.
- **Behaviors:** Purchasing habits, online activity, social media usage, etc.
- **Pain Points:** What problems or challenges do they face that your product or service can solve?
- **Desires and Aspirations:** What are their goals and dreams? How can your offering help them achieve those goals?

The more specific you can be about your target audience, the more effective your marketing and sales efforts will be.

Testing & Refining Your Concept: From Idea to MVP

Once you've gathered market research and identified your target audience, it's time to put your idea to the test. This involves creating a minimum viable product (MVP) - a basic version of your product or service that allows you to gather feedback from potential customers and iterate on your concept.

Here are some ways to test your MVP:

- **Landing Page:** Create a landing page that describes your product or service and includes a call to action (e.g., sign up for a waiting list, pre-order, or request more information).
- **Crowdfunding:** Launch a crowdfunding campaign to gauge interest and gather pre-orders.
- **Beta Testing:** Offer a limited number of people access to your product or service in exchange for their feedback.
- **Social Media:** Use social media platforms to share your idea, engage with potential customers, and gather feedback.

The goal of testing is to learn as much as possible about your target market and refine your concept based on their feedback. Be open to making changes, pivoting your idea, or even scrapping it altogether if the data suggests it's not viable.

Embracing the Entrepreneurial Spirit: Challenge, Innovate, and Adapt

Validation is an ongoing process. Even after launching your business, it's essential to continue gathering feedback, monitoring the market, and adapting your strategies as needed. The entrepreneurial journey is filled with challenges and uncertainties, but by embracing your innovative spirit and being willing to challenge the status quo, you can create a business that thrives in the ever-evolving marketplace.

Here are some key principles to keep in mind:

- **Embrace feedback:** Be open to hearing constructive criticism and use it to improve your product or service.
- **Stay agile:** Be willing to pivot your business model or strategy if necessary.
- **Never stop learning:** Continuously seek out new knowledge, skills, and experiences to stay ahead of the curve.
- **Build a strong team:** Surround yourself with talented individuals who share your vision and can help you bring your ideas to life.
- **Focus on providing value:** Deliver exceptional products or services that solve real problems for your customers.

Remember:

- **Dare to be different:** Don't be afraid to challenge the status quo and offer something unique and valuable to the marketplace.
- **Embrace your innovative spirit:** Let your creativity and passion guide you as you develop and refine your business idea.
- **Stay resilient and adaptable:** The entrepreneurial journey is filled with ups and downs. Be prepared to face challenges, learn from your mistakes, and adapt your strategies as needed.

By following these principles and embracing the spirit of innovation, you can transform your entrepreneurial vision into a sustainable and thriving reality. It's time to unleash your inner fire, challenge the norms, and let your innovative spirit shine!

CHAPTER SIX

Building Your Business Foundation - Explore the depths of your entrepreneurial vision. The possibilities are endless, waiting to be discovered.

"Align your work with your soul, and success will follow"

Laying the Groundwork for Success: Turning Your Vision into a Concrete Plan

You've identified your passions, honed your skills, and validated your business idea. Now, it's time to roll up your sleeves and start building the foundation for your entrepreneurial venture. This chapter will guide you through the essential steps of crafting a business plan, setting SMART goals, and establishing a strong brand identity – the pillars that will support your business as it grows and thrives.

The Blueprint for Success: Crafting a Comprehensive Business Plan

A business plan is more than just a document; it's a roadmap that outlines your vision, strategies, and action steps for achieving your entrepreneurial goals. It serves as a guide for you and a tool for communicating your vision to potential investors, partners, and stakeholders.

Key components of a business plan:

1. **Executive Summary:** A concise overview of your business, including your mission, vision, target market, products or services, and financial projections.

2. **Company Description:** A detailed description of your business, including its legal structure, ownership, history, and key team members.

3. **Market Analysis:** An in-depth analysis of your target market, including its size, demographics, trends, and competitive landscape.

4. **Products or Services:** A clear description of your offerings, their unique features and benefits, and how they solve customer pain points.

5. **Marketing and Sales Strategy:** Your plan for reaching and attracting customers, including your pricing strategy, promotional tactics, and sales channels.

6. **Operational Plan:** The logistics of how your business will operate, including your production processes, supply chain, and staffing requirements.

7. **Management and Organization:** The structure of your management team, their roles and responsibilities, and their relevant experience.

8. **Financial Projections:** Detailed financial forecasts, including your income statement, balance sheet, and cash flow statement, demonstrating the viability of your business.

9. **Appendix:** Supporting documents, such as market research data, resumes of key team members, and legal agreements.

Tips for creating a compelling business plan:

- **Be clear and concise:** Avoid jargon and overly complex language.
- **Focus on your target audience:** Tailor your plan to the specific needs and interests of potential investors or lenders.
- **Highlight your unique value proposition:** Clearly articulate what sets your business apart from the competition.
- **Be realistic and data-driven:** Base your financial projections on solid market research and realistic assumptions.
- **Show your passion:** Let your enthusiasm for your business shine through in your writing.

Remember, your business plan is a living document. It should be updated regularly as your business evolves and you gain new insights.

Setting SMART Goals: Paving the Path to Success

Goals provide direction and focus, helping you stay motivated and track your progress. When setting goals for your business, it's important to make them SMART:

- **Specific:** Clearly define what you want to achieve.
- **Measurable:** Establish concrete criteria for measuring progress.
- **Achievable:** Set goals that are challenging but realistic.
- **Relevant:** Ensure your goals align with your overall business vision and mission.
- **Time-bound:** Set deadlines for achieving your goals.

Examples of SMART goals:

- **Increase website traffic by 20% in the next six months.**
- **Acquire 100 new customers within the first year of operation.**
- **Achieve a 15% profit margin by the end of the second year.**
- **Launch a new product line within 12 months.**
- **Expand into a new market segment within three years.**

By setting SMART goals, you can break down your larger vision into smaller, more manageable steps, making it easier to track your progress and stay motivated along the way.

Building a Strong Brand: Creating a Memorable Identity

Your brand is more than just a logo or a tagline; it's the overall perception that people have of your business. It encompasses your values, your personality, and the experience you provide to your customers.

A strong brand can help you:

- **Stand out from the competition:** Differentiate yourself in a crowded marketplace.
- **Attract and retain customers:** Build trust and loyalty with your target audience.
- **Command premium pricing:** Charge higher prices for your products or services.
- **Increase brand awareness:** Make your business more recognizable and memorable.
- **Attract top talent:** Attract and retain high-quality employees who resonate with your brand values.

Key elements of a strong brand:

- **Brand name:** A memorable and relevant name that reflects your business and resonates with your target audience.
- **Logo:** A visual representation of your brand that is easily recognizable and conveys your brand personality.
- **Tagline:** A concise and impactful phrase that captures the essence of your brand.
- **Brand voice:** The tone and style of your communication, which should be consistent across all channels.
- **Brand story:** The narrative that explains your company's origins, mission, and values.
- **Brand experience:** The overall experience you provide to your customers, from the moment they first interact with your brand to the after-sales support.

Tips for building a strong brand:

- **Be authentic:** Let your brand reflect your true values and personality.
- **Be consistent:** Maintain a consistent brand voice and visual identity across all channels.

- **Focus on customer experience:** Provide exceptional service and create a positive and memorable experience for your customers.
- **Tell your story:** Share your brand story with your audience to build an emotional connection.
- **Engage with your community:** Use social media and other channels to interact with your customers and build relationships.

The Foundation of Your Future: Building a Sustainable Business

Building a strong business foundation requires more than just a good idea and a passion for your work. It involves careful planning, strategic decision-making, and a commitment to continuous learning and growth.

By crafting a comprehensive business plan, setting SMART goals, and establishing a strong brand identity, you're laying the groundwork for a sustainable and successful entrepreneurial venture.

Remember:

- The possibilities are endless.
- Embrace the journey, explore the depths of your entrepreneurial vision, and let your innovative spirit guide you towards a future filled with freedom, purpose, and abundance.

The next chapter will delve into the challenges and rewards of navigating the real world as an entrepreneur. You'll learn how to overcome fear and doubt, master the art of self-discipline, and build a supportive network to help you thrive on your journey.

Part III: Navigating the Real World

- Chapter 7: Overcoming Fear and Doubt

- Chapter 8: Mastering the Art of Self-Discipline

- Chapter 9: Building a Support Network

CHAPTER SEVEN

Overcoming Fear and Doubt - Every ending marks a new beginning. Embrace the unknown with courage and resilience.

"Leave a legacy, not just a paycheck"

Conquering the Inner Saboteur: Navigating the Emotional Landscape of Entrepreneurship

You've laid the groundwork, built a solid foundation, and are ready to step into the real world as an entrepreneur. But as you venture into the uncharted territory of building your own business, you're likely to encounter a formidable foe: fear and doubt.

This chapter is your guide to navigating the emotional landscape of entrepreneurship, equipping you with the tools and strategies to overcome these internal obstacles and emerge stronger, more resilient, and more confident in your pursuit of success.

The Nature of Fear and Doubt: Understanding the Enemy Within

Fear and doubt are natural human emotions, especially when stepping outside your comfort zone and embarking on a new venture. They can manifest in various ways, from subtle anxieties to full-blown panic attacks.

Common fears and doubts that entrepreneurs face:

- **Fear of failure:** The worry that your business won't succeed, leading to financial ruin, embarrassment, or disappointment.

- **Fear of the unknown:** The anxiety of venturing into uncharted territory, not knowing what challenges or obstacles you may encounter.

- **Fear of rejection:** The concern that your ideas, products, or services won't be accepted or valued by the market.

- **Imposter syndrome:** The feeling that you're not qualified or capable enough to run a successful business, despite your skills and experience.

- **Self-doubt:** The nagging voice in your head that questions your decisions, abilities, and worthiness.

These fears and doubts can be paralyzing, preventing you from taking action, making bold decisions, and fully embracing your entrepreneurial potential. However, it's important to remember that these emotions are not unique to you. Every successful entrepreneur has faced them at some point in their journey. The key is to learn how to manage and overcome them.

Identifying and Addressing Your Fears: Shining a Light on the Shadows

The first step to overcoming fear and doubt is to acknowledge their presence. Don't try to suppress or ignore these emotions; instead, bring them to the surface and examine them closely.

Ask yourself:

- What specific fears and doubts are holding me back?
- What are the underlying beliefs or assumptions that fuel these fears?
- What is the worst-case scenario, and how likely is it to happen?
- What can I do to mitigate the risks and increase my chances of success?

By identifying your fears and understanding their root causes, you can begin to develop strategies for addressing them.

Developing Resilience and Mental Toughness: Building Your Inner Strength

Resilience is the ability to bounce back from setbacks, adapt to change, and persevere in the face of adversity. It's a crucial trait for entrepreneurs, who often face unexpected challenges and obstacles on their journey.

Here are some ways to cultivate resilience and mental toughness:

- **Practice mindfulness and self-awareness:** Pay attention to your thoughts and emotions, and learn to recognize when fear and doubt are creeping in.
- **Develop a positive self-talk:** Challenge negative thoughts and replace them with affirmations and empowering statements.
- **Visualize success:** Imagine yourself achieving your goals and overcoming challenges.
- **Focus on your strengths:** Remind yourself of your past accomplishments and the skills and talents you possess.
- **Seek support from others:** Talk to mentors, coaches, or trusted friends who can offer encouragement and guidance.
- **Practice self-care:** Take care of your physical and mental health through exercise, healthy eating, and relaxation techniques.
- **Embrace challenges as opportunities for growth:** View setbacks as learning experiences and use them to fuel your determination.

Strategies for Staying Motivated: Fueling Your Entrepreneurial Fire

Motivation is the driving force that propels you forward on your entrepreneurial journey. It's what keeps you going when the going gets tough, and it's what inspires you to push beyond your limits and achieve your goals.

Here are some strategies for staying motivated:

- **Set clear and inspiring goals:** Define what you want to achieve and create a roadmap to get there.
- **Break down large goals into smaller, achievable steps:** This will make your goals feel less daunting and more attainable.
- **Celebrate your progress:** Acknowledge your achievements, big and small, and reward yourself for your hard work.
- **Surround yourself with positive and supportive people:** Connect with other entrepreneurs, mentors, and friends who believe in you and your vision.
- **Find inspiration in others' success stories:** Read books, listen to podcasts, and attend events that feature successful entrepreneurs.
- **Practice gratitude:** Take time each day to appreciate the good things in your life and the progress you're making.
- **Take care of your physical and mental health:** A healthy body and mind are essential for maintaining motivation and focus.
- **Don't be afraid to ask for help:** When you're feeling overwhelmed or stuck, reach out to your support network for guidance and encouragement.

Embracing the Unknown: Turning Fear into Fuel

The entrepreneurial journey is a path filled with uncertainty. There will be moments of doubt, setbacks, and unexpected challenges. But instead of fearing the unknown, learn to embrace it.

- **View challenges as opportunities for growth:** Every obstacle you overcome will make you stronger and more resilient.
- **Embrace failure as a learning experience:** Don't let setbacks discourage you. Analyze what went wrong, learn from your mistakes, and move forward with renewed determination.
- **Stay curious and adaptable:** Be open to new ideas, feedback, and opportunities. The ability to pivot and adapt is essential for success in the ever-changing business world.
- **Trust your intuition:** Listen to your gut feeling and follow your instincts.
- **Celebrate the journey:** Focus on the process, not just the destination. Enjoy the ride and appreciate the lessons you learn along the way.

Remember:

- **Every ending marks a new beginning.** Let go of the past and embrace the possibilities that lie ahead.
- **Embrace the unknown with courage and resilience.** Face challenges head-on, learn from your experiences, and keep moving forward.
- **Believe in your boundless potential.** You have the power to create your own reality.

In the next chapter, we'll explore the importance of self-discipline in the entrepreneurial world. You'll learn how to develop productive habits, manage your time effectively, and avoid distractions, setting you up for success as you navigate the real world of business.

CHAPTER EIGHT

Mastering the Art of Self-Discipline - Trust in your abilities, take that leap of faith. The journey of a thousand miles begins with a single step.

"Self-discipline is the bridge between dreams and achievements"

Engine of Entrepreneurial Success: Cultivating the Habits and Routines That Drive Results

 In the previous chapters, we delved into the psychological aspects of entrepreneurship, exploring the importance of mindset, self-belief, and overcoming fear and doubt. Now, it's time to shift our focus to the practical side of the equation – mastering the art of self-discipline. This chapter will empower you to cultivate the habits, routines, and strategies that will propel you towards your entrepreneurial goals, one step at a time.

The Power of Self-Discipline: The Key to Unlocking Your Potential

Self-discipline is the ability to control your impulses, resist distractions, and consistently take action towards your goals, even when it's challenging or uncomfortable. It's the bridge between intention and accomplishment, the engine that drives progress and transforms dreams into reality.

In the entrepreneurial world, self-discipline is paramount. Unlike traditional employment, where you have a boss or manager to provide structure and accountability, entrepreneurship requires you to be your own motivator, manager, and cheerleader. Without self-discipline, it's easy to fall prey to procrastination, distractions, and self-sabotaging behaviors.

Building Productive Habits and Routines: The Foundation of Success

Habits are the small, repeated actions that shape our daily lives. They can be either positive or negative, empowering or limiting. Building productive habits is essential for creating a sustainable and successful entrepreneurial lifestyle.

Here are some key strategies for cultivating productive habits:

1. **Start Small and Be Consistent:** Don't try to overhaul your entire life overnight. Instead, focus on making small, incremental changes that you can stick to consistently.
2. **Identify Your Key Priorities:** What are the most important tasks or activities that will move your business forward? Focus your energy and attention on these priorities.
3. **Create a Daily Routine:** Establish a structured routine that includes dedicated time for work, exercise, self-care, and personal pursuits.
4. **Eliminate Distractions:** Minimize interruptions and create a focused work environment. Turn off notifications, close unnecessary tabs, and let others know when you need uninterrupted time.
5. **Use Time-Blocking:** Allocate specific blocks of time for different tasks or activities. This can help you stay focused and avoid multitasking.

6. **Leverage Technology:** Use productivity tools and apps to streamline your workflow, manage your tasks, and track your progress.
7. **Reward Yourself:** Celebrate your wins and acknowledge your progress. Positive reinforcement can help you stay motivated and on track.
8. **Be Flexible:** Life happens, and sometimes your routine will need to be adjusted. Don't beat yourself up if you miss a day or two. Just get back on track as soon as possible.

Time Management and Prioritization: Making Every Minute Count

Time is your most valuable asset as an entrepreneur. Mastering the art of time management and prioritization is essential for maximizing your productivity and achieving your goals.

Here are some effective time management strategies:

1. **The Eisenhower Matrix:** Categorize your tasks into four quadrants based on their urgency and importance:

- **Quadrant 1: Urgent and Important:** Tasks that require immediate attention and have a significant impact on your goals.
- **Quadrant 2: Important but Not Urgent:** Tasks that contribute to your long-term goals but don't have immediate deadlines.
- **Quadrant 3: Urgent but Not Important:** Tasks that demand your attention but don't contribute significantly to your goals.
- **Quadrant 4: Not Urgent and Not Important:** Tasks that are neither urgent nor important and can be eliminated or delegated.

Focus on prioritizing tasks in Quadrant 2, as these are the activities that will truly move the needle in your business.

2. **The Pareto Principle (80/20 Rule):** This principle states that roughly 80% of your results come from 20% of your efforts. Identify the 20% of tasks that generate the most significant results and prioritize them.
3. **Batching:** Group similar tasks together and complete them in one focused session. This can help you avoid context switching and increase efficiency.
4. **Delegation:** Don't try to do everything yourself. Delegate tasks that can be handled by others, freeing up your time to focus on your core strengths and priorities.
5. **Say No:** Learn to say no to requests or opportunities that don't align with your goals or priorities.

Avoiding Procrastination and Distractions: Staying Focused and on Track

Procrastination and distractions are the enemies of productivity. They can derail your progress, sap your motivation, and prevent you from achieving your goals.

Here are some tips for overcoming procrastination and staying focused:

1. **Identify your procrastination triggers:** What situations or tasks tend to lead you to procrastinate? Once you know your triggers, you can develop strategies to avoid or overcome them.
2. **Break down large tasks into smaller, more manageable steps:** This can make them feel less overwhelming and easier to start.
3. **Set deadlines and create accountability:** Give yourself deadlines for completing tasks and share your goals with someone who can hold you accountable.
4. **Use the Pomodoro Technique:** Work in 25-minute focused intervals, followed by a 5-minute break. This can help you maintain focus and avoid burnout.
5. **Eliminate distractions:** Minimize interruptions by turning off notifications, closing unnecessary tabs, and creating a dedicated workspace.
6. **Reward yourself:** Celebrate your wins and acknowledge your progress. This can help you stay motivated and on track.
7. **Practice self-compassion:** Don't beat yourself up if you slip up or have a less productive day. Just acknowledge it, learn from it, and move on.

Remember:

- **Trust in your abilities.** You have the skills, knowledge, and determination to succeed.
- **Take that leap of faith.** Don't let fear or doubt hold you back.
- **The journey of a thousand miles begins with a single step.** Start small, stay consistent, and celebrate your progress along the way.

By cultivating productive habits, managing your time effectively, and avoiding distractions, you'll build the self-discipline necessary to navigate the challenges of entrepreneurship and achieve your goals.

In the next chapter, we'll explore the importance of building a support network as you navigate the real world of business. You'll learn how to connect with mentors, advisors, and peers who can offer guidance, encouragement, and collaboration on your entrepreneurial journey.

CHAPTER NINE

Building a Support Network - Find your tribe, those who uplift and inspire you. Together, we achieve greatness.

"Surround yourself with those who lift you higher"

Beyond the Lone Wolf: The Power of Community and Collaboration in Entrepreneurship

In the previous chapters, we've explored the internal aspects of entrepreneurship, focusing on mindset, self-discipline, and overcoming fear and doubt. Now, it's time to expand our focus outward and recognize the importance of building a strong support network. This chapter will guide you through the process of cultivating relationships with mentors, advisors, peers, and communities that will empower, inspire, and propel you towards your entrepreneurial goals.

The Myth of the Lone Wolf Entrepreneur: Dispelling the Misconception

Popular culture often portrays entrepreneurs as solitary figures, toiling away in isolation, driven by their own ambition and grit. While self-reliance and determination are certainly essential traits, the myth of the lone wolf entrepreneur can be misleading and detrimental.

The reality is that no one achieves success alone. Every successful entrepreneur has a network of supporters, mentors, advisors, and collaborators who have contributed to their journey. Building a strong support network is not a sign of weakness; it's a strategic advantage that can provide you with the resources, guidance, and encouragement you need to thrive.

The Benefits of a Strong Support Network:

- **Emotional support and encouragement:** Entrepreneurship can be a rollercoaster ride, filled with highs and lows. Having a network of people who believe in you and your vision can provide invaluable emotional support and encouragement during challenging times.

- **Knowledge and expertise:** Connecting with mentors and advisors who have experience in your industry or field can provide you with valuable insights, advice, and guidance.

- **Accountability and motivation:** Sharing your goals and progress with others can help you stay accountable and motivated.

- **Collaboration and partnership opportunities:** Building relationships with other entrepreneurs and professionals can lead to collaborations, partnerships, and new business opportunities.

- **Access to resources and opportunities:** Your network can provide you with access to funding, talent, and other resources that can help you grow your business.

- **Sense of community and belonging:** Being part of a supportive community can combat feelings of isolation and provide a sense of belonging.

Mentors and Advisors: Tapping into Wisdom and Experience

Mentors and advisors are individuals who have achieved success in their own fields and are willing to share their knowledge, experience, and insights with you. They can offer guidance, advice, and support as you navigate the challenges of entrepreneurship.

Finding a mentor:

- **Identify your needs and goals:** What specific areas do you need guidance in? What are your short-term and long-term goals?
- **Look for someone who has achieved what you want to achieve:** Seek out individuals who have experience in your industry or field and have a track record of success.
- **Network and build relationships:** Attend industry events, join online communities, and reach out to people you admire.
- **Be clear about your expectations:** Communicate your goals and what you hope to gain from the mentorship relationship.
- **Be respectful of their time and expertise:** Value their insights and be prepared to implement their advice.

Peer Groups and Communities: Finding Your Tribe

Connecting with other entrepreneurs and like-minded individuals can provide a sense of community, belonging, and shared purpose. Peer groups and communities can offer:

- **A safe space to share challenges and successes:** You can openly discuss your experiences, learn from others' mistakes, and celebrate each other's wins.
- **Opportunities for collaboration and networking:** You can connect with potential partners, collaborators, and clients.
- **Access to shared resources and knowledge:** You can tap into the collective wisdom and experience of the group.
- **Motivation and inspiration:** You can draw inspiration from the successes of others and stay motivated on your own journey.

Finding your tribe:

- **Join online communities and forums:** There are countless online groups and forums dedicated to entrepreneurship and specific industries.
- **Attend industry events and conferences:** These events offer opportunities to network, learn, and connect with other entrepreneurs.

- **Join local business organizations or co-working spaces:** These spaces provide opportunities for collaboration and community building.
- **Start your own mastermind group:** Gather a small group of like-minded entrepreneurs to meet regularly, share ideas, and support each other's growth.

The Importance of Collaboration: Building Win-Win Partnerships

Collaboration is a powerful tool for entrepreneurs. By partnering with others, you can leverage their skills, expertise, and resources to achieve mutual success.

Benefits of collaboration:

- **Access to new markets and customers:** Partnering with complementary businesses can help you reach a wider audience and expand your customer base.
- **Shared resources and expertise:** You can pool your resources and knowledge to create something greater than the sum of its parts.
- **Increased efficiency and productivity:** By dividing tasks and responsibilities, you can streamline your workflow and achieve more in less time.
- **Innovation and creativity:** Collaborating with others can spark new ideas and lead to breakthroughs that wouldn't be possible alone.
- **Mutual support and encouragement:** You can provide each other with feedback, advice, and motivation.

Tips for successful collaboration:

- **Choose partners wisely:** Look for individuals or businesses that share your values, vision, and work ethic.
- **Establish clear expectations and communication:** Define roles and responsibilities, set deadlines, and maintain open and honest communication throughout the collaboration.
- **Be flexible and adaptable:** Be willing to compromise and adjust your approach as needed.
- **Celebrate successes and learn from failures:** Acknowledge each other's contributions and use setbacks as opportunities for growth.

Cultivating Strong Relationships: Nurturing Your Network

Building a strong support network takes time and effort. It's about cultivating genuine relationships based on trust, respect, and mutual support.

Here are some tips for nurturing your network:

- **Be a giver, not just a taker:** Offer your help and support to others without expecting anything in return.
- **Stay connected:** Make an effort to stay in touch with your network, even when you're not actively seeking help or advice.
- **Show appreciation:** Express gratitude for the support and guidance you receive from your network.
- **Be a good listener:** Pay attention to the needs and challenges of others and offer support when you can.
- **Celebrate each other's successes:** Share in the joys and accomplishments of your network and offer encouragement along the way.

Remember:

- **Find your tribe:** Surround yourself with people who uplift and inspire you.
- **Embrace collaboration:** Partner with others to achieve mutual success.
- **Nurture your relationships:** Cultivate genuine connections based on trust, respect, and mutual support.

By building a strong support network, you'll create a powerful ecosystem that will empower you to overcome challenges, seize opportunities, and achieve greatness on your entrepreneurial journey.

Part IV: Thriving Beyond the Matrix

- Chapter 10: Financial Freedom

- Chapter 11: Living a Life of Purpose

- Chapter 12: The Journey Continues

CHAPTER TEN

Financial Freedom - The path to abundance is a journey of self-discovery. Seek, and you shall find the keys to unlock your financial dreams.

"Financial freedom is a mindset, not a bank balance"

 **the Paycheck: Embracing a Mindset of Abundance and Prosperity**

In the previous chapters, we've explored the emotional and practical aspects of building a successful business. Now, it's time to delve into the heart of entrepreneurial freedom - financial independence. This chapter will guide you through the journey of cultivating a healthy relationship with money, developing smart financial habits, and creating a sustainable path to abundance.

Redefining Wealth: It's Not Just About the Numbers

Financial freedom is more than just having a large bank account or a high net worth. It's about having the resources and flexibility to live life on your terms, pursue your passions, and make choices that align with your values.

True wealth encompasses:

- **Security and peace of mind:** Knowing that you have enough money to cover your basic needs and weather unexpected financial storms.
- **Choice and flexibility:** The ability to choose how you spend your time, where you live, and what work you do.
- **Generosity and contribution:** The capacity to give back to your community and support causes you care about.
- **Legacy and impact:** Leaving a positive mark on the world and creating a lasting legacy for future generations.

The Mindset Shift: From Scarcity to Abundance

One of the most crucial steps towards achieving financial freedom is shifting your mindset from scarcity to abundance.

- **Scarcity Mindset:** Focuses on limitations, lack, and fear of not having enough. It can lead to hoarding, overspending, and a constant feeling of anxiety about money.
- **Abundance Mindset:** Recognizes the limitless possibilities and opportunities available. It fosters gratitude, generosity, and a belief in your ability to create wealth and prosperity.

Cultivating an abundance mindset involves:

- **Practicing gratitude:** Appreciate what you have and focus on the positive aspects of your financial situation.

- **Visualizing your goals:** Create a clear mental picture of your financial dreams and imagine yourself achieving them.
- **Affirming your abundance:** Use positive affirmations and self-talk to reinforce your belief in your ability to create wealth.
- **Surrounding yourself with positive influences:** Connect with people who have an abundance mindset and support your financial goals.
- **Taking inspired action:** Take steps towards your financial goals, even if they seem small at first.

Mastering Money Management: Building a Solid Financial Foundation

Building a solid financial foundation is essential for achieving long-term financial freedom. It involves developing smart money management habits, tracking your income and expenses, and creating a budget that aligns with your goals.

Key principles of money management:

- **Track your income and expenses:** Know where your money is coming from and where it's going. Use budgeting tools or apps to help you stay organized.
- **Create a budget:** Allocate your income towards your essential expenses, savings goals, and discretionary spending.
- **Live below your means:** Spend less than you earn and avoid lifestyle inflation.
- **Pay off debt:** Prioritize paying off high-interest debt, such as credit cards or personal loans.
- **Build an emergency fund:** Set aside 3-6 months' worth of living expenses in a readily accessible savings account.
- **Automate your finances:** Set up automatic transfers to your savings and investment accounts to make saving effortless.

Investing for the Future: Growing Your Wealth

Investing is a powerful tool for building long-term wealth and achieving financial freedom. It allows your money to work for you, generating passive income and growing your net worth over time.

Key principles of investing:

- **Start early:** The earlier you start investing, the more time your money has to grow through compound interest.

- **Diversify your investments:** Don't put all your eggs in one basket. Spread your investments across different asset classes to reduce risk.
- **Invest for the long term:** Avoid trying to time the market or chase short-term gains. Focus on building a diversified portfolio that will grow steadily over time.
- **Seek professional advice if needed:** If you're unsure where to start or need help managing your investments, consider working with a financial advisor.

Creating Multiple Streams of Income: Diversifying Your Financial Portfolio

Relying on a single source of income can be risky. By creating multiple streams of income, you can diversify your financial portfolio and reduce your dependence on any one source.

Some potential income streams for entrepreneurs:

- **Your primary business:** The core product or service you offer.
- **Passive income streams:** Investments, rental properties, royalties, online courses, etc.
- **Freelancing or consulting:** Offering your skills and expertise on a project basis.
- **Affiliate marketing:** Promoting other people's products or services and earning a commission on sales.
- **E-commerce:** Selling physical or digital products online.

By diversifying your income streams, you can create a more resilient financial foundation and increase your overall earning potential.

The Journey of Self-Discovery: Aligning Your Finances with Your Values

Achieving financial freedom is not just about accumulating wealth; it's also about aligning your finances with your values and priorities.

This involves:

- **Defining your financial goals:** What do you want to achieve with your money? Do you want to travel the world, retire early, or support charitable causes?
- **Creating a spending plan that reflects your values:** Allocate your resources towards the things that matter most to you.
- **Avoiding impulse purchases and lifestyle inflation:** Be mindful of your spending habits and avoid getting caught up in the comparison trap.

- **Giving back to your community:** Support causes you care about and use your financial resources to make a positive impact on the world.

Remember:

- **Seek, and you shall find:** The keys to unlocking your financial dreams are within your reach.//
- **Embrace the journey:** The path to financial freedom may not always be easy, but it's worth it.
- **Celebrate your progress:** Acknowledge your achievements, big and small, and use them as motivation to keep moving forward.

By embracing an abundance mindset, mastering money management, investing wisely, and creating multiple income streams, you can build a solid financial foundation and achieve the freedom and flexibility you desire.

In the next chapter, we'll explore how to live a life of purpose by aligning your business with your values and making a positive impact on the world.

CHAPTER ELEVEN

Living a Life of Purpose - Embrace your unique talents and passions. Craft a life that resonates with your soul and leaves a positive mark on the world.

"Never stop learning, never stop growing"

 **Profit: Finding Fulfillment and Meaning in Your Entrepreneurial Journey**

In the previous chapters, we've explored the practical and financial aspects of building a successful business. Now, it's time to delve into the heart of what truly makes entrepreneurship meaningful: living a life of purpose. This chapter will guide you through the process of aligning your business with your values, making a positive impact on the world, and finding true fulfillment in your work.

The Quest for Meaning: Beyond the Pursuit of Profit

While financial success is undoubtedly important, it's not the sole measure of a fulfilling life. True happiness and satisfaction come from living a life of purpose, where your work aligns with your values and contributes to something greater than yourself.

As an entrepreneur, you have the unique opportunity to create a business that reflects your passions, your beliefs, and your desire to make a difference. By aligning your work with your purpose, you can:

- **Experience greater fulfillment and joy:** When you're doing work that matters to you, it doesn't feel like a chore. It becomes a source of inspiration, motivation, and deep satisfaction.

- **Attract loyal customers and employees:** People are drawn to businesses that have a clear purpose and positive impact.

- **Build a sustainable and resilient business:** A purpose-driven business is more likely to weather challenges and thrive in the long run.

- **Leave a lasting legacy:** By contributing to the world in a meaningful way, you can create a legacy that extends far beyond your own lifetime.

Aligning Your Business with Your Values: The Compass for Your Journey

Your values are the guiding principles that shape your beliefs, attitudes, and behaviors. They represent what's most important to you in life and how you want to interact with the world.

By aligning your business with your values, you can:

- **Create a sense of authenticity and integrity:** When your business reflects your values, it feels genuine and true to who you are.

- **Attract customers and employees who share your values:** People are more likely to support and engage with businesses that align with their own beliefs.

- **Make decisions that are consistent with your purpose:** Your values can serve as a compass, guiding you towards choices that are in line with your mission and vision.
- **Build a strong and positive company culture:** When your team shares your values, it creates a sense of unity, collaboration, and shared purpose.

Making a Positive Impact: Using Your Business as a Force for Good

Entrepreneurship offers a powerful platform for making a positive impact on the world. Whether it's through creating innovative solutions to social or environmental problems, supporting local communities, or promoting ethical business practices, you can use your business as a force for good.

Ways to make a positive impact:

- **Incorporate social responsibility into your business model:** Consider how your products or services can benefit society or the environment.
- **Support charitable causes:** Donate a portion of your profits or offer your services to organizations that align with your values.
- **Create a positive workplace culture:** Foster a supportive and inclusive environment for your employees.
- **Promote sustainable practices:** Minimize your environmental impact and operate your business in an ethical and responsible manner.
- **Use your platform to advocate for change:** Speak out on issues that matter to you and use your influence to create positive change.

Finding Fulfillment and Happiness: The True Measure of Success

Ultimately, the goal of entrepreneurship is not just to achieve financial success, but to create a life that is rich in meaning, purpose, and happiness.

Here are some key principles for finding fulfillment and happiness in your entrepreneurial journey:

- **Prioritize your well-being:** Take care of your physical, mental, and emotional health. Make time for self-care, exercise, and relaxation.
- **Cultivate strong relationships:** Nurture your connections with family, friends, and loved ones. These relationships provide support, love, and a sense of belonging.
- **Pursue your passions outside of work:** Make time for hobbies, interests, and activities that bring you joy and fulfillment.

- **Practice gratitude:** Appreciate the good things in your life and focus on the positive aspects of your journey.

- **Give back to your community:** Find ways to contribute to the world and make a positive impact on others.

- **Live in the present moment:** Don't get so caught up in chasing future goals that you forget to enjoy the present.

- **Embrace the journey:** Entrepreneurship is a lifelong learning process. Embrace the challenges, celebrate the victories, and never stop growing.

Remember:

- **The path to abundance is a journey of self-discovery.** Explore your passions, identify your values, and align your business with your purpose.

- **Embrace your unique gifts.** You have something special to offer the world. Share your talents and make a difference.

- **Craft a life that resonates with your soul.** Live authentically, pursue your passions, and create a life that fills you with joy and meaning.

By following these principles and embracing the power of purpose, you can build a business that not only thrives financially but also nourishes your soul and leaves a positive impact on the world.

CHAPTER TWELVE

The Journey Continues - The future is a blank canvas, waiting for your masterpiece. Embrace growth, adapt to change, and evolve into the entrepreneur you're meant to be.

"The future is yours to create, go beyond the matrix"

 the Horizon: Embracing Lifelong Learning and Growth

Congratulations! You've embarked on an incredible journey, breaking free from the matrix, building a business aligned with your passions, and crafting a life of purpose. But the adventure doesn't end here. In fact, it's just beginning.

This final chapter is a reminder that entrepreneurship is a lifelong journey of learning, growth, and evolution. The future is a blank canvas, waiting for you to paint your masterpiece. Embrace the challenges, celebrate the victories, and never stop striving to become the best version of yourself.

The Importance of Lifelong Learning: Fueling Your Entrepreneurial Fire

In the fast-paced and ever-changing world of business, continuous learning is not just an option, it's a necessity. To stay ahead of the curve, adapt to new technologies, and remain competitive, you must commit to a mindset of lifelong learning.

Here are some strategies for cultivating a learning mindset:

- **Read books and articles:** Stay abreast of industry trends, new technologies, and best practices by reading books, articles, and blogs related to your field.

- **Attend workshops, seminars, and conferences:** Network with other professionals, gain insights from industry leaders, and learn about the latest developments in your field.

- **Take online courses and certifications:** Expand your skillset and knowledge base by enrolling in online courses or pursuing certifications relevant to your business.

- **Seek out mentors and advisors:** Learn from the experiences of those who have already achieved success in your field.

- **Experiment and try new things:** Don't be afraid to step outside your comfort zone and explore new ideas and approaches.

- **Reflect on your experiences:** Take time to analyze your successes and failures, and extract valuable lessons from each.

Remember, learning is not just about acquiring new information; it's about applying that knowledge to improve your business, your skills, and your life.

Adapting to Change: Thriving in a Dynamic World

The only constant in the business world is change. New technologies emerge, consumer preferences shift, and economic conditions fluctuate. The ability to adapt to change is crucial for entrepreneurial success.

Here are some tips for navigating the ever-changing landscape:

- **Stay informed:** Monitor industry trends, economic news, and technological advancements that could impact your business.
- **Be flexible and agile:** Be willing to pivot your strategies, adapt your business model, and embrace new opportunities as they arise.
- **Cultivate a growth mindset:** View challenges as opportunities for learning and growth, rather than setbacks.
- **Build a resilient team:** Surround yourself with adaptable and resourceful individuals who can help you navigate change.
- **Embrace innovation:** Continuously seek out ways to improve your products, services, and processes.

Remember, change is inevitable. By embracing it and adapting proactively, you can turn challenges into opportunities and ensure your business remains relevant and successful.

Evolving as an Entrepreneur: The Journey of Personal and Professional Growth

Entrepreneurship is not just about building a business; it's also about personal and professional growth. As you navigate the challenges and triumphs of running your own venture, you'll inevitably evolve and transform as an individual.

Here are some key areas of growth to focus on:

- **Leadership:** Develop your leadership skills to inspire and motivate your team, build strong relationships, and make effective decisions.
- **Communication:** Hone your communication skills to clearly articulate your vision, connect with your audience, and build trust with customers and stakeholders.
- **Problem-solving:** Enhance your problem-solving abilities to identify and address challenges creatively and effectively.
- **Decision-making:** Learn to make informed and decisive choices, even in the face of uncertainty and risk.
- **Emotional intelligence:** Cultivate self-awareness, empathy, and the ability to manage your emotions and build healthy relationships.
- **Resilience:** Develop the mental and emotional strength to overcome setbacks, persevere through challenges, and bounce back from failures.

Remember, growth is a continuous process. Be patient with yourself, celebrate your progress, and never stop striving to become the best version of yourself.

The Future Awaits: Painting Your Masterpiece

As you continue on your entrepreneurial journey, remember that the future is a blank canvas, waiting for your masterpiece. The possibilities are endless, and the opportunities for growth and impact are boundless.

Embrace the journey, stay curious, and never stop learning. Cultivate a mindset of abundance, adaptability, and resilience. Surround yourself with a supportive network of mentors, advisors, and peers.

Most importantly, never lose sight of your purpose. Let your passions and values guide your decisions, and use your business as a force for good in the world.

By following these principles and embracing the spirit of lifelong learning and growth, you can create a business and a life that is truly fulfilling, impactful, and uniquely yours.

Conclusion

Your Reality Awaits - Unleashing Your Entrepreneurial Spirit and Leaving a Legacy.

"The greatest risk is not taking one"

Embracing Your New Life: Stepping into Freedom and Fulfillment

Throughout this book, we've journeyed together through the complexities of the 9-to-5 matrix, exploring its limitations, challenging its norms, and ultimately, discovering the path to a life beyond its confines. We've delved into the power of mindset, the importance of self-discovery, the art of validation, the discipline of building a business foundation, the resilience needed to navigate the real world, the pursuit of financial freedom, the alignment with purpose, and the continuous pursuit of growth.

Now, as we reach the culmination of this journey, it's time to celebrate the transformation you've undergone and the boundless possibilities that await you. You are no longer a passive participant in the matrix; you are an empowered creator, ready to shape your own reality.

A Life of Freedom and Choice

Imagine waking up each morning with a sense of excitement and purpose, eager to tackle the day ahead. Imagine having the freedom to set your own schedule, work from wherever you choose, and pursue projects that ignite your passions. Imagine being in control of your income, your time, and your destiny.

This is the life that awaits you beyond the matrix. It's a life where you're not just building a business, but crafting a lifestyle that aligns with your values, your dreams, and your authentic self. It's a life where you're not just earning a living, but making a meaningful impact on the world.

The Ripple Effect: Inspiring Others to Break Free

Your journey to entrepreneurial freedom doesn't end with your own success. It's also about inspiring and empowering others to break free from the matrix and create their own realities.

As you share your story, your passion, and your knowledge, you become a beacon of hope for those who are still trapped in the 9-to-5 grind. You show them that there's another way, a path less traveled, but one that leads to greater fulfillment, purpose, and abundance.

By sharing your journey, you can:

- **Challenge limiting beliefs:** Help others question the status quo and see beyond the illusions of the matrix.
- **Offer guidance and support:** Provide practical advice and mentorship to aspiring entrepreneurs.

- **Build a community of change-makers:** Connect with like-minded individuals who are also striving to create a better world.
- **Leave a lasting legacy:** Inspire future generations to pursue their dreams and make a positive impact.

The Journey Never Ends: Embracing the Adventure of Entrepreneurship

While this book marks the end of one chapter, it's also the beginning of a new and exciting adventure. The entrepreneurial journey is a lifelong process of learning, growth, and evolution.

As you continue to build your business and navigate the real world, remember:

- **Stay curious:** Never stop exploring, learning, and expanding your horizons.
- **Embrace change:** Be adaptable and open to new ideas and opportunities.
- **Cultivate resilience:** Challenges are inevitable, but they can also be opportunities for growth.
- **Nurture your network:** Surround yourself with supportive people who believe in you and your vision.
- **Give back:** Use your success to make a positive impact on the world.
- **Celebrate your wins:** Acknowledge your achievements, big and small, and enjoy the fruits of your labor.
- **Never give up on your dreams:** The path to success may not always be easy, but with passion, perseverance, and a clear vision, you can achieve anything you set your mind to.

Your Reality Awaits: Embrace the Possibilities

The future is yours to create. It's a blank canvas, waiting for your masterpiece. Embrace the freedom, the challenges, and the endless possibilities that lie ahead.

Step into your power, unleash your entrepreneurial spirit, and paint a life that is vibrant, meaningful, and uniquely yours.

Resources

Fueling Your Entrepreneurial Journey.

"One person, with unwavering determination, can spark a movement and change the world"

Congratulations on completing the main chapters of "Beyond the Matrix"! You've gained valuable insights, strategies, and inspiration to break free from the 9-to-5 and build a business that aligns with your passions and values.

But the learning doesn't stop here. To support your continued growth and success as an entrepreneur, I have compiled a curated list of resources that will further fuel your journey.

This chapter is your treasure trove of knowledge, offering a wealth of information, tools, and communities to help you navigate the exciting world of entrepreneurship. From books and articles to online courses and podcasts, these resources will empower you to expand your skills, stay informed about industry trends, connect with like-minded individuals, and continue your lifelong learning journey.

Remember, the path to entrepreneurial success is paved with continuous learning, adaptation, and growth. So, dive into these resources, explore the vast landscape of knowledge, and equip yourself with the tools you need to thrive in the ever-evolving world of business.

Books:

- **Mindset: The New Psychology of Success** by Carol S. Dweck: This groundbreaking book explores the power of mindset and how it can shape our beliefs, behaviors, and ultimately, our success.

- **The Lean Startup** by Eric Ries: This essential guide introduces the lean startup methodology, a scientific approach to building and managing startups that emphasizes experimentation and validated learning.

- **The 4-Hour Workweek** by Timothy Ferriss: This controversial yet inspiring book challenges traditional notions of work and offers strategies for creating a lifestyle of freedom and flexibility through entrepreneurship.

- **Zero to One** by Peter Thiel: This thought-provoking book explores the importance of innovation and creating something truly new, rather than simply copying existing ideas.

- **The E-Myth Revisited** by Michael E. Gerber: This classic book debunks the myths surrounding entrepreneurship and provides a practical framework for building a successful business.

- **Atomic Habits** by James Clear: This practical guide offers a proven framework for building good habits and breaking bad ones, essential skills for any entrepreneur.

- **Start with Why** by Simon Sinek: This inspiring book explores the power of purpose and how it can drive success in business and life.

- **The $100 Startup** by Chris Guillebeau: This book showcases inspiring stories of individuals who built successful businesses with minimal investment, proving that entrepreneurship is accessible to everyone.

- **Rich Dad Poor Dad** by Robert Kiyosaki: This personal finance classic challenges traditional views on money and wealth and offers insights into building financial independence through entrepreneurship and investing.

- **The Hard Thing About Hard Things** by Ben Horowitz: This candid and insightful book offers practical advice for navigating the challenges and complexities of entrepreneurship.

Articles and Blogs:

- **Entrepreneur.com:** A leading online resource for entrepreneurs, offering news, advice, and inspiration on a wide range of topics related to starting and growing a business.

- **Forbes Entrepreneurs:** A section of Forbes dedicated to entrepreneurship, featuring articles, interviews, and profiles of successful entrepreneurs.

- **Inc.com:** Another popular online resource for entrepreneurs, providing insights, strategies, and tools for building and managing a business.

- **Harvard Business Review:** A prestigious publication offering in-depth articles and research on business and management topics, including entrepreneurship.

- **Seth Godin's Blog:** Renowned marketer and author Seth Godin shares his insights on marketing, leadership, and creativity on his popular blog.

- **The Tim Ferriss Show:** A popular podcast featuring interviews with world-class performers from diverse fields, offering valuable lessons on productivity, business, and personal development.

- **Smart Passive Income:** A blog and podcast by Pat Flynn, sharing strategies for building online businesses and generating passive income.

- **The School of Greatness:** A podcast by Lewis Howes, featuring interviews with successful entrepreneurs, athletes, and thought leaders, offering inspiration and practical advice for achieving greatness.

Online Courses and Learning Platforms:

- **Coursera:** A platform offering online courses from top universities and institutions worldwide, covering a wide range of topics relevant to entrepreneurship, such as business, marketing, finance, and technology.

- **Udemy:** A marketplace for online courses, offering a vast selection of affordable courses on various subjects, including entrepreneurship, business skills, and personal development.

- **Skillshare:** A platform for creative learning, offering online classes and workshops on topics like design, marketing, photography, and more.

- **LinkedIn Learning:** A platform offering video courses taught by industry experts on a variety of business and technology topics.

- **MasterClass:** A platform featuring online classes taught by world-renowned experts in their respective fields, including business, leadership, and creativity.

Communities and Networking:

- **Local business organizations and chambers of commerce:** Connect with other entrepreneurs in your local community, attend networking events, and access resources and support.

- **Co-working spaces:** Share a workspace with other entrepreneurs and freelancers, fostering collaboration and community.

- **Online forums and communities:** Join online groups and forums dedicated to entrepreneurship and specific industries to connect with like-minded individuals, share ideas, and get support.

- **Meetup.com:** Find and attend local events and meetups related to your interests and industry.

- **Social media:** Connect with other entrepreneurs and professionals on platforms like LinkedIn, Twitter, and Facebook.

Tools and Resources:

- **Business planning software:** Tools like LivePlan, Bizplan, and Enloop can help you create a professional business plan.

- **Project management tools:** Platforms like Asana, Trello, and Monday.com can help you stay organized and manage your tasks and projects effectively.

- **Financial management tools:** Apps like QuickBooks, Xero, and FreshBooks can help you track your income and expenses, create invoices, and manage your finances.

- **Marketing and social media tools:** Platforms like Hootsuite, Buffer, and Canva can help you manage your social media presence and create engaging content.

- **Website builders:** Platforms like Wix, Squarespace, and WordPress can help you create a professional website for your business.

Remember:

The resources listed here are just a starting point. As you progress on your entrepreneurial journey, you'll discover additional tools, communities, and learning opportunities that resonate with you and support your specific needs and goals.

Stay curious, keep learning, and never stop exploring the endless possibilities that await you beyond the matrix. The world is your canvas, and the future is yours to create.

www.ingramcontent.com/pod-product-compliance
Lightning Source LLC
Chambersburg PA
CBHW070211230526
45471CB00002B/919